TERRIFIC TEAMS

Meet the SAN FRANCISCO 49ERS

PERCY LEED

Lerner Publications ◆ Minneapolis

Stats in this book are accurate through the 2024 National Football League season.

Lerner Publications Company
An imprint of Lerner Publishing Group, Inc.
241 First Avenue North
Minneapolis, MN 55401 USA

For reading levels and more information, look up this title at www.lernerbooks.com.

Main body text set in ITC Avant Garde Gothic Std.
Typeface provided by Adobe Systems.

Editor: Annie Zheng **Designer:** Mary Ross **Photo Editor:** Elena Mai
Lerner team: Sue Marquis

Library of Congress Cataloging-in-Publication Data

Names: Leed, Percy, 1968- author.
Title: Meet the San Francisco 49ers / Percy Leed.
Description: Minneapolis, MN : Lerner Publications , 2026. | Series: Lerner sports rookie. Terrific teams | Includes bibliographical references and index. | Audience: Ages 5–8 | Audience: Grades K–1 | Summary: "The San Francisco 49ers are the tenth-oldest team in the NFL. From superstar players to thrilling wins, learn more about the history of the team nicknamed The Niners"— Provided by publisher.
Identifiers: LCCN 2024045862 (print) | LCCN 2024045863 (ebook) | ISBN 9798765668474 (library binding) | ISBN 9798765683705 (paperback) | ISBN 9798765681930 (epub)
Subjects: LCSH: San Francisco 49ers (Football team)—History—Juvenile literature.
Classification: LCC GV956.S3 L44 2026 (print) | LCC GV956.S3 (ebook) | DDC 796.332/640979461—dc23/eng/20241118

LC record available at https://lccn.loc.gov/2024045862
LC ebook record available at https://lccn.loc.gov/2024045863

Manufactured in the United States of America
1-1011742-53815-3/14/2025

Photo Acknowledgments
MediaNews Group/The Mercury News/Getty Images, p. 5; Sundry Photography/Alamy, p. 7; George Rose/Getty Images, p. 9; Michael Zagaris/San Francisco 49ers/Getty Images, pp. 11, 20; AP Photo/David Durochik, p. 13; AP Photo/Ric Tapia, p. 14; AP Photo/Jeff Lewis, p. 16; AP Photo/Brooke Sutton, p. 19; Michael Owens/Getty Images, p. 22; AP Photo/Tom DiPace, p. 23.
Design elements: Kwangmoozaa/Getty Images; Andrii Shelenkov/Getty Images; AnthiaCumming/Getty Images.
Cover: AP Photo/Kevin Terrell.

Table of Contents

★ CHAPTER 1 ★

The Niners

Quarterback Brock Purdy handed the ball to teammate Deebo Samuel. Samuel ran to the end zone. Touchdown!

The San Francisco 49ers became a team in 1946. They have won the Super Bowl five times.

Their nickname is The Niners.

In 2014, the team moved to Levi's Stadium in Santa Clara, California.

★ CHAPTER 2 ★

Big Moments

San Francisco played their first Super Bowl in 1982. They beat the Cincinnati Bengals 26–21.

In 1990, the 49ers beat the Denver Broncos 55–10. It is the biggest win in any Super Bowl.

The 49ers played a close game against the New Orleans Saints in 2019. San Francisco won 48–46.

In 2024, the 49ers became champions of their conference. They beat the Detroit Lions 34–31.

★ CHAPTER 3 ★

Best Players

Quarterback Joe Montana was a great leader. He led the 49ers to four Super Bowl wins.

Jerry Rice was one of the best wide receivers ever. He holds the NFL record for most career catches with 1,549.

Running back Frank Gore spent 10 seasons with the 49ers. He is number three in the NFL for career rushing yards with 16,000.

Terrell Owens was a great 49ers pass catcher. He once caught 20 passes in a game.

Nick Bosa is one of the top defenders in the NFL. He won the 2022 Defensive Player of the Year award.

George Kittle is a star tight end.
He has been to six Pro Bowls.

★ CHAPTER 4 ★

The Faithful

Fans of the San Francisco 49ers are nicknamed The Faithful. They stay by the team's side through good and bad seasons.

San Francisco is next to San Francisco Bay. Many Niners fans wear shirts that say, "Faithful to the Bay."

Christian McCaffrey

The team has many of the best players in the NFL.

Two of them are Fred Warner and Christian McCaffrey.

The 49ers are ready to win more games.

SAN FRANCISCO 49ERS TEAM LEADERS

Passing touchdowns:	Joe Montana, 244
Passing yards:	Joe Montana, 35,124
Receiving touchdowns:	Jerry Rice, 176
Rushing yards:	Frank Gore, 11,073
Rushing touchdowns:	Joe Perry, 68

Glossary

bay: a body of water connected to a larger body of water such as a sea or lake

conference: one of two groups of teams in the NFL

NFL: National Football League

Pro Bowl: the NFL's all-star game

Learn More

Downs, Kieran. *Football*. Bellwether, 2024.

Huddleston, Emma. *Get Ready for a Football Game*. Bearport Publishing, 2024.

Leed, Percy. *Football's Super Bowl*. Lerner Publications, 2025.

Index